Do-It-Yourself Brand Design

Make Logos, Ads and Everything in Between

Gabrielle Weinman

Dedication

For all my heroes that inspire me to pay it forward.

#tweet

Table of Contents

Introduction | vii

Chapter 1 — Start Here | 01

Chapter 2 — Logos 101 | 11

Chapter 3 — Embrace Graphic Standards | 21

Chapter 4 — Creative To-Do List | 31

Chapter 5 — Advertising Basics | 45

Chapter 6 — Find It Here | 53

About the Author | 59

Introduction   Hello

A lot of great books will tell you how to start a small business. I've read a hefty stack of them. They're all packed with bits of wonderful advice, from business plans to budgeting. However, when describing how to design a small business brand and advertise it, I found them light on real-world advice. That inspired me to share some of the best insights I've come across.

Years of hands-on work as a creative professional for myriad companies, from big time corporations to small non-profits, has taught me many things. This little illustrated book is an efficient way to consider your options and get inspired. Use it as a reference guide every step of the way. It's quick and to the point by design. You have a new brand to launch and no time to waste.

So whether you want to do it all yourself or hire some help I've got suggestions for you. Plus, there are tons of new creative and production options available online now. I'd be thrilled if you'd allow me to share the best of everything with you.

Gabrielle Weinman
Designer, Creative Director, Author, CEO and Doodler

Chapter 1   Start Here

When I was a kid my mom gave me excellent advice, "You only get one chance to make a great first impression. So don't blow it." Little did she know that's also the secret to success in branding a business as well as making new friends in the sandbox.

When people look at your new logo for the first time, read your ad or visit your website can they relate? Or do they say, "You're not for me. No thanks"? I want people to say, "Yes! Your product is perfect for me! Tell me more."

"How do you eat an elephant? One bite at a time." Ok, please don't actually eat him, how horrible! The point here is doing something that feels too big to tackle, like creating a new brand from scratch, can feel a tad overwhelming. Break it down into small bite-size steps and you will make progress and conquer the big task sooner than you think. This book is a series of bite-size steps that will help get the job done.

Building your roadmap. Before we take the first step toward branding your business, is your business plan written? If so, great. Skip to the next section. If not, write one now.

A business plan defines your goals, strategies and how you plan on making money. It describes how your business will be structured and financed, and how manufacturing and sales would work.

Modern
Minimal
Martinis

Good Karma
Good Friends
Good Times

If it's a service business your employees are your treasured assets. How will the company be run and organized? It's like a resume for your new business. You'll need this business plan to help guide your decisions during the brand creation process.

Create a clear picture of your dream customers. Think about your future customers often during this process to make sure your new logo design or ad campaign suits them.

Make a visual picture of who you're selling your product to. Start by tearing photos out of magazines that reflect who your customer is and what they care about. Focus on people, color, words and images that remind you of those customers. Look at all the samples together and step back into their shoes. Does the assortment of images and words represent them? Does it feel like whom you intend to talk to? Take away the bits that don't fit. Make a note of why you think the examples do connect with your customers. The better you can visualize your happy customers, the better you can speak their language.

Please note that "everyone" is not your customer. It rarely works to talk to everyone unless you have the Coca-Cola mega global marketing budget. Instead please be as specific as you can. A clear picture will focus your branding and advertising dollars the smartest way possible.

The sample collection of images and words on the left hand page represents dream customers for a unique giftware business called Gratitude Cocktail. The customers are defined as: *"A woman who connects with a higher power and to whom spirituality isn't all fire and brimstone. She is filled with gratitude, positive energy and enjoys drinks with good friends. She's not ashamed to admit she loves the Holy Spirit —and a few distilled ones."* Compare that definition and the images and words. They connect.

Here's a fun fact: Top strategic branding firms and advertising agencies charge big bucks for something similar to this assortment of images and words. The fancy name for it is a "mood board." You just saved money making your own. Isn't that nice.

Imagine what your new brand could look like. Start looking more closely at other brands you admire for style clues. For example, compare the clean and modern look of Apple computer ads to the down home, cozy look of the local pie shop menus. Does either feel right for your brand? Collect anything that connects. Tear out magazine ads, collect business cards, menus, paint swatches, anything as long as the object reflects your new brand image.

When your creative brief is murky or vague, that's exactly the kind of work you'll get back. Guaranteed.

Why you need to start with a creative brief. You can't build a house without blueprints; same goes for designing your brand. Ok, you can go without blueprints but it's messy and your chance of making expensive errors rises dramatically. A good creative brief will help focus your energy, time and budget at every stage of the branding process. You'll save countless hours of frustration for you and anyone who is working with you if everyone is reading from the same roadmap.

I'm passionate about the creative brief because it works. It's so much easier to try out different ideas at this stage. If something does not feel right on paper, rewrite it and it costs you nothing.

Now for the good news! All of the ideas, notes, images, magazine ads, business plans and other samples you have collected so far will help to write this creative brief. The research has already started. Once this brief is completed you can celebrate and get the creative process rolling.

If you are hiring a graphic designer or creative agency, give them a copy of your final creative brief and your dream customer photo collage. Not only is it helpful in explaining your assignment, the detail it provides helps estimate costs and timing for your job much more easily. Or, if you are going to do all the work by yourself, be sure to refer back to this often before making any design decisions. The best creative products come from clear and focused briefs.

www.YourNameHere.com

Is the website address for your new business name available? Check by typing it into your web browser. Next, Google your business name to see if any other businesses already exist with that name.

Don't get discouraged if the web address is taken. Try a variation by abbreviating it. Your search results may also tell you that a business just like yours already exists with the same name. It's better to know now before spending time and effort only to have a future conflict looming.

Specialized websites can help you find options and buy an available website address. GoDaddy.com, one of many great resources, makes it easy, fast and free to do research. When you find the web address you want, buy it on their site and you will officially own it.

How to Write
A Creative Brief

What's the business objective?

Refer to your business plan for specific goals and objectives that apply here. How will you measure the success of your new brand design and advertising? Consider any unique opportunities or challenges. Define the results you want for your brand as it grows.

What's your brand personality?

If your brand was a person, what words could you use to describe him or her? The options are endless but your list should not be. Pick the top five traits on your list and rank them in order, from top to bottom. Not sure? Judge one word against another directly, which is better? Pick that word. Repeat using all the words on the list to get the final five. Clear descriptions lead to stronger creative solutions.

innovator
maverick
emotional
INDULGENT
stylish
expert
humble
bold
modern

Who's your customer?

The photo and words collage exercise helps envision your customer. Now define the vivid details in words here. Beyond the basics of your customer's age or gender are many useful clues that can help you communicate. Describe your customer's daily life to see how your product fills a need. Is she in need of fast service? Does he have a passion or belief that transcends age?

What's the idea?

This is the heart of the assignment. The more focused the better the creative. Try not to cram five different things in here. Write one sentence that describes your brand idea. If you are hiring a designer or creative agency they'll help come up with this idea for you so write "TBD" here for now.

What's on the Creative To-Do list?

The top of the Creative To-Do list usually starts with a logo and brand colors. That's followed by everything that needs your spectacular new logo and brand messages applied. It's a lot of stuff to make, so write it all down in this section. On the next page you'll find a helpful checklist for reference. Feel free to edit or add to it to make it your own.

List everything in this section to get the big picture. You can always add or delete stuff; don't worry, this list is not set in stone. Just because you can, does not mean you need to create everything at once. Often it's better to start with the basics, then test and learn.

The To-Do list will show you and everyone involved in the creative process the scope of the job. Prioritize what must be ready day one of your business opening its doors. Then list what can be created later if you need to break it into a few phases to better manage your cash flow and time.

Creative Checklist:

At the very top, four must-have items.

- ❏ Logo
- ❏ Tagline or No Tagline
- ❏ Brand Colors & Typefaces
- ❏ Brand Copy Tone & Visual Style
- ❏ Business Cards
- ❏ Email Template
- ❏ Website & Mobile Site
- ❏ Stationery & Forms
- ❏ Store Signage
- ❏ E-commerce Store
- ❏ Search & Google Adwords
- ❏ Print Ad
- ❏ Outdoor Ad
- ❏ Radio Ad
- ❏ Social Media
- ❏ Branded Shirts, Hats, Mugs & More
- ❏ And the list goes on, keep 'em coming.

What's the timing?

It's best to list the dates you know of here and be realistic. If you are hiring a designer or creative agency they can give you a ballpark estimate based on this creative brief. If you are doing all the work on your own, it's just a little extra homework reaching out to individual print, web or media vendors to check on individual timelines.

ASAP is not an ideal timeline. You can move quickly but you risk errors and omissions and that costs more money if you have to redo something. Go ahead and start plugging the different dates into a master list in calendar order.

> Budget and Timing are closely related.
> One drives the other.

What's the budget?

Ideally, your business plan should have a creative or marketing budget in it. If not, don't worry, you can get free individual cost estimates and add them up. In chapters four and five I share resources for producing everything on the Creative To-Do list.

If you have a leisurely timeline, sometimes you can get a better deal. Or, if you are on the ASAP timeline you may pay expensive ASAP rush prices. Consider a "phased" approach. I encourage you to create essentials in small quantities during phase one or when you first open your doors for business. For example, test one hundred brochures or printed pieces to see if you love them or need to make a change before you buy ten times as many. This also helps to plan for expenses in phases so you don't use the entire budget on day one.

That's it.

This final creative brief is the best way to manage everyone's expectations, especially your own. Parts of the brief could evolve as the creative process unfolds. That's ok. Update it and keep going.

Heal the Bay, a non-profit in Los Angeles gave me the chance of a lifetime. They wanted a logo design and the simple creative brief idea was: "Keep garbage out of the Santa Monica Bay to save it." Over twenty years later, this hard working logo design is going strong. I still get a thrill when I see it on a jogger's T-shirt. The point of this story is to reinforce how awesome a great creative brief is. Without that simple idea for inspiration this logo may never have seen the light of day.

Chapter 2   Logos 101

Individual colors, images and typefaces have unique personalities. Take advantage of picking the right ones and you'll have a successful logo design. Whether designing it yourself or hiring a graphic designer, the process for creating one is basically the same.

Do-it-yourself logo designers, I salute you. Dreaming up strategic ideas and computer software programs are basics you'll need. Adobe InDesign is a great graphics software for print because looking at multiple typefaces is quick and easy.

Start the logo design process by looking at your business name in as many different typefaces as possible. Adobe Type allows you to enter your sample business name text and view it in their fonts at Adobe.com. With thousands of typefaces to choose from, look for examples that reflect your brand personality.

When adding an image or icon to the type design, step away from the computer. Keep it simple with hand-drawn sketches at first; use black felt-tip markers and blank copier paper. Personally, I draw one logo image idea in the middle of each page. That way I can quickly sort what I like and pin the contenders up on a wall. Try out many ideas quickly without getting too invested in them. The trouble with drawing on the computer right away is that you could spend a long time perfecting an idea that goes nowhere. Don't waste your precious time.

Cut up the printouts of your business names in different typefaces, and tape them up next to your logo designs. It's a fast way to see if anything works. Compare one design to another. Which feels right in your gut? Discard the weak designs. This comparison test is a recurring theme in creative development and how design professionals work. It filters out the stinkers fast. You'll see I use it again and again.

Classic fonts never go out of style:

Helvetica

Gill Sans

Futura Extra Bold

Garamond

Bodoni

To make a logotype unique, "tweak it." Without a special something it's possible your logotype could blend into the crowd. Add small graphic touches with symbolic meaning to make it your own. Modify one or more of the letters or make the first letter a larger size and you have just customized or tweaked it. Try a distinctive background shape behind the logotype. There are many ways to go. Customizing the typeface helps make your logotype one of a kind.

Pictures are easy to remember. If I showed you ten famous iconic logos without the names, I'll bet you'd guess every one of them. (Quick: Golden Arches. Yep. McDonald's.) Many people are visual creatures; they may not remember a name, but they sure do remember the picture. Many large companies add a logo, photo or graphic icon to their logotype to help people remember their brand. A well-designed logo also gives a nice graphic element to use in your communications and will make your business look even more unique and professional.

Adobe Photoshop and Illustrator are software programs used to create the final logo art. Designing icon logos can be a challenge if you are not great at drawing or using graphics software. Sticking to a type-only logo may be the best way to go if that's the case.

Make sure you can read the logotype in many sizes. When considering design options, look at the same logotype in small and large sizes. Business cards and websites often need small logos, while store signs or bus bench ads may need a large one. You can quickly see if a design option can pass this test.

A great exercise to help figure out if a logo finalist is perfect for you is to look at it on a business card, a webpage, store sign or package design. Do it yourself and cut out different size logos and place them on top of another business card or webpage printout to get a fast look. This helps visualize your brand and gets you to think about the pieces you need to design next.

Hire a graphic designer. Not everyone wants to design their own logo. You may have a graphic designer already lined up. Another option is to post an online description of your job for a small fee, and get proposals back from logo designers. Elance.com is one site that connects people with online designers. Be sure to look at the designer's portfolio carefully. Read comments left by previous customers. Notice that the hourly fees and bids vary greatly. A super low price may sound great, but be sure the designer can deliver the quality you need. You may get bids from all over the world. Be sure that there are no language barriers that could derail your progress.

What Color Is Your Brand?

The meanings of some colors are obvious. Red hearts equal love. Flashing red lights mean danger. Other colors have more subtle meanings, even gray has meaning.

Since every color has a personality, pick the perfect color to match your brand and it works harder for you. If you want to be a rebel and use an unusual color, that's fine; just be aware of what meaning that color may hold for others. Have fun exploring the meaning and big brand colors in the blocks that follow.

Red is:

excitement
youthful
bold
love
passion
romance
danger
energy

Target
Coca-Cola
CNN
Nintendo
Pinterest
KFC
Nabisco
Exxon

Orange is:

friendly

cheerful

confidence

innovation

creativity

thinking

ideas

Amazon

Hooters

Harley Davidson

Blogger

Nickelodeon

Shutterfly

Yellow is:

optimism

clarity

caution

intellect

friendliness

warmth

National Geographic

Chevrolet

Denny's

McDonald's

Hertz

Nikon

Green is:

peaceful
freshness
nature
growth
money
health
life

Whole Foods
John Deere
Girl Scouts
Starbucks
Land Rover
British Petroleum
Animal Planet

Blue is:

trust
peace
sincerity
dependable
strength
confidence
integrity

Twitter
American Express
Volkswagen
Facebook

Purple is:

creative
wise
royalty
luxury
wisdom
dignity
imaginative

Taco Bell
Barbie
Yahoo!
Hallmark
Cadbury
Syfy Channel
T-Mobile

Gray is:

balance
neutral
authority
maturity
security
stability
calm
tranquility

Apple
Wikipedia
Honda
Mercedes-Benz

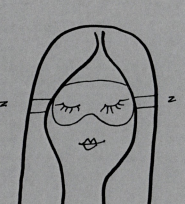

17

> Use your brand color everywhere; it's an easy way to extend your brand's presence.

Picking colors. The best way to judge color is to look at all the different color logo designs on white backgrounds. Like before, use the "comparison test." Judge one against another and narrow finalist color logos to three to five. Next, apply them to a business card or webpage design. Does it look great there too?

Plan ahead. You might need a logo to sit on top of a colored or dark background. Take a look at the logo designs in all white on top of the color background you are considering. Now, which logo looks great everywhere?

Check the creative brief again. My hope by now is that you have the creative brief in your hand and are reading it aloud before selecting your winning logo design. Consider all the finalists up on the wall and then one by one ask:

Does it help solve the business objective?
Does it match the five brand personality words?
Does the design and color feel relatable to customers?
Does it feel like the right logo for all of your communications?
If the answer to all of the above questions is "yes," great work! If not, weed out the weak logos and keep going.

Before you fall in love. Do a fast and free online search to see if your logo design is already out in the world. Let Google Images search for you: http://images.google.com/. Upload the logo image file (TIFF or JPEG) for an instant visual search on the web for anything that is remotely similar. If the search does not reveal obvious conflicts you are in a great place. Hopefully you've just avoided the unpleasant surprise of seeing someone beat you to the same exact logo design.

Ask your unofficial focus group for their thoughts. Find your focus group of friends, neighbors or anyone that resembles your new customers and ask what they think about your logos. Be careful. If your mom is not your target customer, please show someone else. This is the cheapest and fastest way to get a quick read on the design options. My rule of thumb is if I hear the same negative feedback about an idea from three people out of ten, I may move on to a different option. If one objects and the other nine people give you a thumbs up you may be on to something big. You'll never please everyone, so don't try.

Big identity and logo design firms use fancy focus groups or online surveys at this point to determine the same thing. Savvy startups with small budgets get similar information without paying thousands in consultant fees. Getting feedback now is important; your logo needs to serve you well for years. Spending a few days, at this point asking future customer types if they can relate to it is totally worth it.

You have a winner! All the steps are checked off and you have a final logo design. Congratulations. Make it official and trademark or register your logo now. If you have a small local business you may be ok skipping this step. If you aim to to grow into a large business, or want to sell a product or service online, you should consider filing for a trademark.

I trusted my brand trademarking assignment to a helpful trademark lawyer based on a recommendation from my business partner. The lawyer told me that once the application is submitted to the United States Patent and Trademark Office the wait is long; it can take over a year. But as long as the paperwork was filed, your logo is somewhat protected even during the long approval process.

It is possible to fill out the government application forms yourself online. However, if you are not a lawyer I'd suggest you skip this option. I gave it my best shot. After a day wasted reading page after page of confusing instructions at the United States Patent and Trademark Office website (uspto.gov) I happily went to plan B, mentioned above.

Chapter 3   Embrace Graphic Standards

We see hundreds, if not thousands, of brand images a day. It would be a miracle if we remembered half of them. Successful companies know this and work hard to be memorable. Be consistent with your brand look and message, and you'll have a greater chance of being memorable, too.

Spend some time documenting everything you just worked so hard to create. Make a "graphic standards" document that shows the do's and don'ts of using your logo. It also shows your colors with specifications for using them. Never leave these basics up to chance. Working with a printer or web designer, or designing anything yourself, goes much smoother when graphic standards are figured out first.

From billboards to business cards, everything needs to be designed with a consistent look, feel and message. If the website looks totally foreign to the sign in the front of the store, that's a missed opportunity to make a connection. Plus, customers have more confidence in a well-designed business or brand when they see its visual design consistent everywhere they look. That's good for business.

Sample graphic standards in the pages that follow are meant to demonstrate what to expect from this document I'm recommending for you. Customize the details and make a new version for your business. See how Gratitude Cocktail, the giftware business mentioned in chapter one, embraces graphic standards in the following pages.

Graphic standards help communicate a consistent brand image. Gratitude Cocktail logos and colors used consistently help customers find and follow our brand. That's why it's important to review and apply the guidelines in this manual.

Company Overview

A brand is at its best when it helps others, which is why we insist Gratitude Cocktail revolves around positive messages for women. Our "gratitude with attitude" approach has built a strong emotional relationship by creating things that help women connect with the higher power in their lives by sharing laughs, insights and gentle reminders to be good to oneself.

Contents

The Logo 23
The "Signature" 24
Unacceptable "Signature" Forms 25
The Colors 26
The Typefaces 27
Business Communications 28
Product Applications 29

The Logo

Use this logo alone or with its companion logotype. If used alone we prefer that the logotype appear somewhere on the web or printed page to help identify the brand. Ideally, the area around the logo is clear with no text or distracting backgrounds touching it. This logo may be used in black or white on contrasting color backgounds.

COLOR

The "Signature"

Combining a logo and logotype in an specific arrangement creates the official company "Signature." This defines the preferred combination of the elements, including the trademark symbol. Provide both color and black and white high-resolution digital art files in JPEG and EPS file formats for use. Everyone on your design and production team can use this "Signature" to keep the brand consistent everywhere it appears.

BLACK & WHITE

Unacceptable "Signature" Forms

Worst case scenario examples help others see what to avoid. There's no way to show every bad example, so just cover the most likely misuses of the company "Signature."

Avoid a one-color logotype and only use approved colors, please.

Don't substitute any typefaces for the logotype, and please avoid ALL CAPS.

Don't break the logotype into two lines or place the logo on the bottom.

The Colors

The offical brand colors are purple, black and blue and are represented in the color swatches below. Additional secondary colors may be used if they don't clash with these brand colors. Detailed production specifications are also below to help accurately reproduce the colors from print to computer screens.

PURPLE

Solid Color Printing:
Pantone 2577

Four Color Printing:
Cyan 40%
Magenta 45%
Yellow 0%
Black 0%

Computer Screen Color:
Red 156
Green 141
Blue 195

BLACK

Solid Color Printing:
Black

Four Color Printing:
Cyan 0%
Magenta 0%
Yellow 0%
Black 100%

Computer Screen Color:
Red 0
Green 0
Blue 0

BLUE

Solid Color Printing:
Pantone 319

Four Color Printing:
Cyan 52%
Magenta 0%
Yellow 19%
Black 0%

Computer Screen Color:
Red 113
Green 203
Blue 210

The Typefaces

These two options were chosen because they are timeless, easy to relate to and fit our brand's character. Other typefaces might look similar, but please no substitutions. Large headlines and small body copy both look great in these typefaces (some call them fonts; it's the same thing).

Garamond Premier Pro

abcdefghijklmnopq
rstuvwxyz 1234567890
ABCDEFGHIJKLMNOP
QRSTUVWXYZ

Helvetica Neue Light

abcdefghijklmnopq
rstuvwxyz 1234567890
ABCDEFGHIJKLMNOP
QRSTUVWXYZ

Business Communications

We are a fun brand and our business communications reflect that. Please feel free to pick up on these design cues when creating new marketing materials from print ads and packaging to website designs.

Business Card

e-Newsletter Template

Product Applications

We're open to using the logo in creative ways that break a few rules as long as it fits our brand character. The greeting card design below is a good example of an exception to the logo rules. Even though a graphic is touching the edge of the logo it works in this specific example.

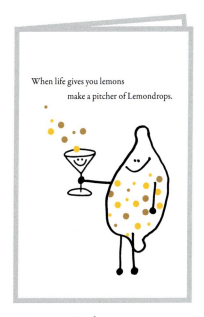

When life gives you lemons
make a pitcher of Lemondrops.

Product Hangtag   Greeting Card

| Chapter 4 | Creative To-Do List |

Back in the late nineties some people thought the new World Wide Web was a fad. I dove in head first and bet my career that it was going to be awesome. People told me I was nuts, but something about it just made sense to me. No self-respecting print art director walked away from working on Lexus automotive brochures and ads to make websites and web banners. Did she?

Yes, and committing "career suicide" did pay off. Years later the Internet became a big deal, and I now use the strengths of both old and new media, as needed. My love and respect for logo design, print, billboards or the "traditional advertising" stuff continues to play a big role. Add digital to the mix and the number of places to speak to your customer is whole a lot bigger.

That's why I feel uniquely qualified to give you advice on the expansive Creative To-Do list options before you. From creative theory to technology solutions, I'm sharing years of experience that works.

Grab that list. Look back at the creative brief section called "Creative To-Do List." Is the list of items your business needs still the same? Update the list if it's changed. It feels good to cross the first few things off, like having the logo finished. Done. Next. Hooray!

Get free production estimates for costs and timing. By doing the upfront work in previous chapters you should be in good shape and have the basic information for the rough estimates you now need.

Collect your creative brief, graphic standards, customer photo collage and research about websites you admire, to give others detailed info for estimates. The bids you get back will be much more accurate when you supply those details up front.

Get a realistic timing estimate on all items so you can coordinate everything being produced on one common timeline. Getting the costs estimated will allow you to prioritize projects within your budgets.

Pictures and graphics need to be a part of your rough production estimates, too. Most people forget about these early on. Even though you have not started your brochure or web designs yet, it's a good idea to set aside some money to pay for a few images. If you are lucky enough to be a good photographer or illustrator and make your own, congratulations!

There are great low-cost options like iStock.com. Many of their stock images can be purchased for a few dollars. It's usually cost effective to repeat images on both your website and brochures to save on image buying costs. I don't advise that you "grab" images off of the web for final use. If the picture is ever identified by the owner you may have to pay a fine and change your materials, too.

Sign up for great email deals. Several of the online resources I'm going to tell you about have one thing in common. If you go to their sites and sign up for their free email newsletters you will probably get a thank-you message that includes a discount for your first order. Many of them give you another future discount when they ship you your first order, as well. Take my advice and sign up, wait a day or two, and you'll see discounts in your inbox for items you will be buying anyway. Everyone loves to save money.

Creative Theory for Do-It-Yourselfers
Part One: Business Cards to Websites

If there was a formula for "being creative" I'd be the first to give it to you. Thinking up clever ideas based on solid strategy takes some work. It's frustrating right up until you think of the perfect idea, then it's an amazing high of happiness and success.

Find idea inspiration. Before you can design anything you need a plan. Look at examples of visual design you admire and also relates nicely to your creative brief. Look at the samples you've already collected. You need inspiration to start dreaming up new ideas.

Have fun. Draw a lot of rough design ideas quickly, at first. Spread them out and compare them. It's the same "comparison test" as described in the Logos 101 chapter. Pick things you like, take the weak ones away, and then add more options. When you are having fun it shows, and the work is usually better. If you get stuck, go on to something else, the solution may come to you later out of the blue. Just don't lose it, write it down. When you go back to your design you'll have a new solution to try.

Keep it simple. The more stuff you add to your layout the harder you make the viewer work. A few well-chosen words or images is the most effective way to go. It's tempting to fill all the space, but don't.

Use a grid. Especially when using type in a layout, simple alignment of copy and images guides your reader's eye to the important details. Without a simple grid you have chaos.

Use YouTube to learn new software. When I need to master a new graphics software feature I search for video tutorials. There's a ton to choose from on YouTube.

There are more online options today for producing quality materials at a great price than ever before. My favorites are mentioned here, but feel free to search out more. There are endless ways to go.

Business cards and stationery

For a majority of businesses digital printing options look great and are pretty inexpensive. It's easy to upload a custom design, or most offer many pre-designed templates.

Good online providers like Vistaprint.com and Overnightprints.com will be happy to send you printed samples by regular mail, so you can see and feel the quality for yourself before you order. Plus, these printers can create small quantities first to make sure the design works perfectly for you. That way, you don't commit to ordering five thousand business cards only to realize the design is not working out as you had hoped.

Fine letterpress business cards or stationery is pricey but it works if you need a polished or luxurious business personality. Eggpress.com has a great reputation. For over ten years they have created beautiful work for small companies and large, well-known brands like Herman Miller and Nike.

For the most cost-effective business cards ever, print your own in small batches. Avery paper company sells a product called Clean Edge Business Cards. One sheet of 8.5" x 11" card stock goes through your color inkjet printer and makes 8 cards each. The business cards pop out easily with clean edges. Very slick. The only downside is that the printer ink will run if the printed cards get wet. An issue if you plan on doing business in or around water.

Forms

There's a very good chance your small business will choose the convenience of digital forms. QuickBooks from Intuit is one option for creating and tracking invoices, estimates, purchase orders and more. There is a customization feature built in that allows you to add your company logo to each of them. It's one more small way to give your documents professional polish.

Email templates

Many businesses are walking away from sending mailers and postcards completely. It's more expensive to print and mail something than sending a well-crafted email to customers. The additional benefit is that email puts your customer one click away from buying a product on your website. You will also be able to see how many people opened and clicked on the email and learn what messages motivate people to buy.

MailChimp.com is one of several user-friendly email service provider options. Many people like the easy-to-use interface and the fast account setup. Once you set up an account, your customer email list is saved for future emails. That's convenient.

Stickers, mugs, pet tees and so much more

Digital printing is exploding with possibilities. Whether you need 2 or 200 mugs with your logo, CafePress.com and Zazzle.com are just two examples that can help with that. If you need a few promotional items they are fantastic resources. Not only do they custom print logos and designs on basics like mouse pads, if you need a tote bag, pet T-shirt or water bottle, they have that too.

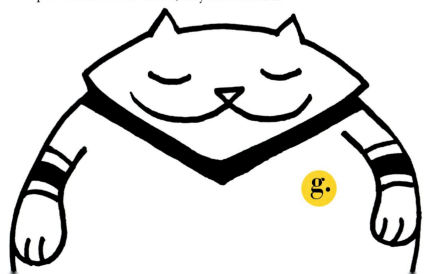

Visit their web galleries for inspiration; new objects to customize are added all the time. Online ordering is simple. Just upload your logo art or design, view the result and click OK to order.

"Starter" Packaging

Instead of ordering expensive, custom-printed shopping bags or shipping boxes right away, save some money. Be creative and buy a few blanks and put nicely designed logo stickers on your bags and packages. Test them out first to see if it's the right size or material for your needs.

Once you run out and need ten times more, it may be time to get the logos printed on them. By then you'll know if the size or paper is right and can confidently order your new custom-printed packages.

Websites, Mobile & Tablets

The range of options available to you could fill an entire book. However the focus here is on fast, smart and inexpensive options for small business startups. Websites start at free and can go up to thousands of dollars to create. The more fancy the features, the higher the price.

Before you hire a web designer, think about what will be on your website. List sections you'll need and what may be in them. Surf your competitors' websites, and see what functions you admire and what you don't. Make a note of exactly what you like, you'll be learning from others' successes. All of this detailed info helps your description for a final website bid or content plan. If you hire professionals they will make plenty of recommendations for you, as well. Don't worry. You can get a more accurate bid and timeline this way, so why not?

Free! It's free! In a few hours you can build a beautiful web and mobile site for free on Weebly.com or Squarespace.com. Designing with their templates is easy and you don't need to be a programmer. The design options offered are beautiful and easily customized. They use "Responsive Design," which means your website looks good on smartphones and tablets too. This feature makes sure you look professional everywhere.

You can build your site and fill it with information, a blog, social media links, YouTube videos and even "light" e-commerce. There is a small monthly fee if you use your business web address instead of the free option that includes weebly plus your name in the web address.

It's easy to play YouTube videos inside your web pages, which saves you money by not paying monthly fees for video hosting. Just set up a free channel for your business on YouTube. Having your business videos on YouTube is another way people can find you when searching keywords. Win win. If you would rather have the videos hosted, or "live on" your web pages, for a few dollars a month more, you can.

You are the Do-It-Yourself designer, writer, blogger, photographer, store manager, website stat tracker and social media team. While you are saving money with free stuff, you are now spending a lot of your time creating and maintaining the content. Factor this into your time and budget. If this sounds like too much work, don't worry there are more ways to go.

Help is here. That free option sounds great, but if there is no way you can or want to do it yourself, that's ok. For a little over $100 a month you get professional help creating and maintaining your web and mobile sites with Web.com. Send them your creative brief, graphic standards, and notes about features you like on other sites as a good example of what you want. Websites can be 5 or 500 pages. Get the most complete bid possible to avoid wasted time or money. Pick one of their pre-designed templates and they'll work with you to write and create the first 5 pages for free. The new copy they'll write for you will be "optimized" and show up in search results from Google to Bing.

The monthly fee also includes free emails to the first 250 people in your customer database. They'll connect all your social media links or get a blog set up. They can also help you buy your business web address (URL) and give you access to your web tracking stats. When you have updates or changes just call them and they'll make them for you for an additional fee. While you are locked into this monthly fee, you have the benefit of having a professional team to help you.

One-time investment. If you want a professionally designed website and can make your own updates, hire a web designer. After your one-time website design and setup costs, you'll only need to pay for web hosting, which is typically less than ten bucks a month for a small business website.

Wordpress.com and Joomla.com are both excellent "content management platforms," which just means they are designed to be easily updated by non-programmers like you and your staff. You'll need to hire a programmer to set it up for you before you can get started. There is some light coding required. It's important to make updating the information on the website something you or someone on your staff can easily do.

Terrific Wordpress and Joomla programmers for hire can be found on a site called elance.com. Take a good look at the designer's portfolio. Do their past work samples feel like a good fit for your business? Do they have good feedback? Even though you are hiring them remotely there are plenty of ways to check out their past work. For a few bucks you can put your web design job on the site and web design experts will bid on your job.

Savvy storefronts. Want to find new customers? Set up a shop in the world's largest online marketplaces, like ebay.com and etsy.com. Both have easy online tools to set up shop in a few hours; no programming required. Ebay alone has over a hundred million visitors a month searching for products. If you sell handcrafted or vintage products, Etsy is a great place to set up shop with over ten million visitors a month to their shopping portal.

Both sites provide sophisticated buying functions that determine shipping and taxes and can take payments by credit card or Paypal. And they both charge a small percentage on each sale. You're saving money by not paying to build a sophisticated shopping website; this trade-off could be attractive for some. Link to your online store from your website. It may not be the most elegant solution on the planet, but it's effective. For those on a tiny budget, this is an affordable way to have a store in a marketplace of millions.

The finest money can buy. Hire a digital agency if you need a complex website built from scratch. It takes a digital village to make big brand websites simple to use and gorgeous.

Information Architects create website plans to make finding stuff easy. Content strategy and creative people develop the words and images you need. Search experts make your website easy for search engines to find. Social media experts and digital media buyers help customers connect with you. Check out topinteractiveagencies.com for recommendations, or just search "best digital agencies."

Social Media

Many businesses thrive by "having conversations" with their customers on Facebook, Twitter, Pinterest and other social sites. Friends tell more friends, and news of a great product can spread quickly without spending money on ads.

Build a loyal fan base by being a business that both talks and listens to its customers. Other people will notice and appreciate that too. Think about how your customers may use social media; not everyone does. Or they favor one kind over another. A big Pinterest fan may have no interest in Twitter. If you are not sure, talk to several customers or future customer types and ask what they use and how they use it. That informal survey could help focus efforts wisely.

Employees who are knowledgeable about your products make great candidates for updating social media sites with news and tips. Since they're wired already, college-age employees are often asked to help monitor daily social media activity as part of their jobs. It does not matter who you choose as long as they visit your social pages a few times a day to monitor the conversations for good or bad comments.

To be a success you'll be spending time updating and adding to these pages. If you can't commit to keeping them up to date, I'd recommend you hold off on joining up. A Facebook page or Twitter feed that is set up and never updated is a bad reflection on your business. Large businesses often employ full-time companies to do their social media listening and use special software programs to monitor conversations automatically. I'm assuming you are doing it on your own for now, but if you grow really fast you might want to look into that option in the future.

Posting plans. Here's a tip for staying on top of your social media posts. At the start of every month, look one month ahead on the calendar and create some posts ahead of time. Make a list of both major holidays and less known ones related to your business. Have any events or sales on the calendar? Then write a clever post and get a picture ready. When that day arrives, post it and look effortlessly smart and relevant. For example, if I had a cupcake shop, I'd be sure to plan a post for National Chocolate Day every year. It might inspire a promotion to get more customers to buy chocolate cupcakes that day too. You can always add posts as they come to mind, but this tip takes the pressure off of coming up with a new one every few days.

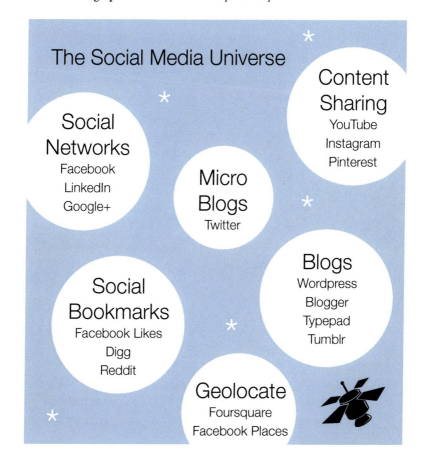

Expect the unexpected. Planning ahead for an unexpected negative post makes good business sense. Don't feel bad, you can't always please everyone. A cool head and time to word a response beforehand makes a fast reply easier to manage. You can always build this list over time, too. Responding quickly to a negative post can have a positive outcome, as well. People are impressed by businesses that respond honestly and promptly. And it earns more loyalty, too.

Facebook

College kids in Massachusetts, USA, were the first to use Facebook to keep up with friends and make new ones. Now people of all ages, from all over the globe, have joined. Many big brands and celebrities have set up pages to communicate with their fans. Interesting to note, now lots of parents have also joined which, in turn, has turned off many kids who have moved on. Not everyone is an automatic Facebook fan.

Easily set up an individual Facebook page, upload your logo and an nice big feature photo. Add the story of your business and contacts on the info page. And don't forget to add a link to your Facebook page from your website. Then start uploading photos, videos and news posts letting folks know what's going on in your world. I'd encourage you to post nice graphic photos on your news feed; they help grab attention and get more "likes" and comments added. Multiple research reports have confirmed this on brands I have worked on. In general, mornings tend to be a good time for posts when people are having their first cup of coffee and checking up on friends.

YouTube

Those businesses lucky to have a product or service that makes for entertaining videos should absolutely start a YouTube channel. Setup is fast and free. Upload your videos, logo and a description of your business and you are ready to go. People often use YouTube as a search engine to find answers to questions and look for news in video form.

Even if you plan on having the same videos on your website, I encourage you to post them and take advantage of all of the traffic

YouTube gets daily. As I mentioned earlier in the website design section, there is an added bonus for you. Your website can pull the videos from YouTube using their awesome technology for free. That means you are not paying for monthly video web hosting and can rely on YouTube's dependable web delivery service.

Twitter

Short messages. Seriously short. The entire message cannot be more than 140 characters. That's actually a good thing; you'll be forced to get to the point. Brands have to work to be relevant. Hard-sell messages don't work. People tune out that sort of thing. But if you share a one-day-only offer or interesting news about your business, that makes loyal fans happy to get the inside scoop. Setup is fast and free. Just upload your logo, describe your business and start tweeting.

Pinterest

"Picture sharing" is a good description of Pinterest. Anyone can tag or "pin" an online photo for friends to see. Some organize their images by subjects and color palettes, kinda like old-fashioned scrap books updated for our new digital age. Brides love to use it for planning their dream weddings. Foodies like to pin yummy dishes from recipes. Some fashion or furniture brands are a perfect fit for Pinterest and have large followings. However, not all brands are right. I can't imagine a lugnut manufacturer is going to have the same loyal Pinterest following as one that sells handmade shoes.

And there's more. Instagram puts cool filters on your smartphone camera so you can take retro style photos and share with friends. Vine-videos.com specializes in making and sharing 7-second video clips. With attention spans shrinking daily, 7-seconds is a manageable length for most people. Google+ is like Facebook but, as of this writing, has not been the same huge success yet. I'm sure there will be another new social sensation soon. Test them all and see what is right for you.

Be Real

One taste
and they
could be
yours

Chapter 5   Advertising Basics

Think about your customers' average day. Where do they spend time? What are they doing? And where can you put ad messages they'll notice? The daily habits of your customers help determine what types of ads will find them out in the world. Once you do find them, be real and use your authentic brand voice in ads to start winning them over. If you need a reminder, look back at the creative brief you wrote. It defined your brand personality and your customers. Along with your business goals it's the guide to making your ads.

Advertising needs fresh ideas, copy, offers and graphics often because messages can grow stale and not work as well after being viewed a few times. I know small businesses don't have the luxury of huge corporate advertising budgets. This chapter is not the ad playbook for big Fortune 500 companies, however, anyone can benefit from some things the big guys have discovered to attract new customers without spending a fortune.

If you can only afford one thing, do this. Advertise online without making a traditional ad. Some of the biggest brands I worked on spent 60-75% of their online advertising budgets on search marketing. It's because search works. Both SEO (search engine optimization) and Google Ads use keywords and phrases your customers will be searching for and make up the foundation of your search copy. Being clear is more important than being clever. The length of the copy is super short and keeps you focused on just a few well-chosen words.

It's easy to buy "Google AdWords" search ads from the biggest player in the online search business. There's free support help to get an account started online at google.com/adwords, or by calling the 800 number. Start small with a few dollars, then watch the progress of your search campaign on your Google AdWords online dashboard. Change ads or try new keywords pretty easily. Track the dates your ads are running and see if you are getting more sales or website visits then.

If you want help, hire an outside freelance SEO search expert who will write "optimized" copy for your website or Google ads. Check out the search marketing talent for hire at elance.com. Be sure to read their job history and comments from past client feedback to see if they are a good fit for you. Many experts on the site are outside the US, so please make sure you speak the same language.

Embrace Yelp. Created to help local businesses, from hair stylists to mechanics, find new customers, it quickly grew in visitors and categories covered. If your business has a physical address you should probably be on Yelp.com. Over 47 million customer reviews are posted. The more positive reviews you have the higher your business ranks in search results. That's great for business. Tell your best customers to write a review and support you. Plus, setting up your page is free.

Go local. Keep advertising costs reasonable by advertising on local radio, billboards or bus benches. Creating your own ads is an option but you have lots of homework before you even start thinking about the creative part. Specifications, final art sizes and formats all vary by each individual ad space you buy. It's a lot more complicated, time consuming and expensive than buying an online search ad.

First call the local radio station or contact sales at outdoor-ad placement companies. They will walk you through some options. They can also share details of the types of people their ads reach. If you need help with your ad message, some companies have in-house creative and production for you for an additional fee.

Creative Theory for Do-It-Yourselfers
Part Two: Making Ads

Looking for inspiration? Start with the "What's your idea?" strategy statement from the creative brief. Write it down on that blank piece of paper before you. Then rewrite it like you would say it to a friend. Or imagine you only have 10 seconds while riding down an elevator. Quick! What would you say to sell your product before the door opens and the nice lady is gone?

Don't be fancy. When you are talking to friends you probably don't use big fancy words. Your ad shouldn't either. Don't write like your prim old English professor talks unless you're selling prim old-fashioned quill pens. Your ad copy should have the same personality as your product.

Keep it short. The less words you use the better. It's less stuff to process when people glance at your ad. You are lucky to get them to look at an image or read a headline as they are flipping through a magazine. People look at pictures and don't read ad copy very often. Remember, people buy magazines for the articles, not the ads. By creating a clutter-free ad you have a better chance of standing out in a sea of other ads crammed with wall to wall stuff.

Lose the tagline. There is no law that says you have to have a tagline. In fact, skipping it is one less item to distract in your ad. Sure, big brands use them, but 95% of taglines are not memorable. And, worse, they can sound vague and distract from your ad message.

Before you go. While taglines are optional, your logo is not. Small businesses should always include a website address or contact info with the logo so customers can find you.

More than you want to take on? It's ok, help is here. Read

Freelance talent. Hire creative freelance professionals who will work hard for your brand like it's their own. As a small business you could be the dream client they're looking for who wants "award-winning" and effective creative work. Compared to hiring an ad agency, it's a deal.

A freelance copywriter and art director who work together are called a "creative team"; they read your creative brief and deliver ideas for ads. Then they help oversee their production. The range of talent and experience is all over the map. The old saying "you get what you pay for" applies here. Talented people with terrific track records charge accordingly, so check out their creative work portfolios and rates first. Word of mouth is a good way to find these folks. Ask other business owners whose ads you admire, who was the creative. Or, try a search for "freelance art director" or "freelance copywriter" on LinkedIn.com.

Narrow focus. Magazines cover every topic under the sun. These niche magazines are laser focused on specific customers, from knitting to nursing. There is a magazine for everyone. If you're lucky to have a business with a small but passionate audience, specific trade or hobby magazines are a great place to advertise. Small space ads are affordable and you'll be talking to people with a passion for your business. Amazon.com/magazines has indepth navigation by categories. Some publications may help you create an ad, or you may want to hire freelance talent mentioned above to make your print ad.

Blog. Attract new fans and customers by blogging about your product or business. Some small businesses skip paid advertising all together and use blogging and social media as an effective way to get the word out. Not all businesses have the perfect content for this approach, but if you are a good fit it's an inexpensive way to attract more customers. There is an added time commitment to consider; writing great blog content takes time to research and develop. Either host the blog on your website or start a free blog at Tumblr or Blogger.

> You deserve every ad option available, but I must caution you about a few.

Avoid ad banners. Even though I have created online ad banner campaigns for cars and cruise vacations I'm not recommending them to you now. For a small business the return on investment is not great. Ad industry data reports that customers click on ad banner messages an average of only .03%. Animated ad banners also need to be created in at least eight sizes to fit everywhere. It can add up. Most hire a digital design team and a producer or project manager to keep track of them, get banner ads placed and track the results coming back.

In addition, keep in mind more people are surfing the web on their smartphones AND web banners don't work on them. Mobile ads are actually different types of banners than web ads. It's a lot of work for a .03% reward. However, no two businesses are alike. Ad banners could be perfect for your specific business and now you know what to look out for.

Junk mail is a great name for it. No one I know looks forward to getting snail mail ads from businesses they don't know stuffed in their mail boxes. Save some trees and money. A much better way to go is to build an email list. Ask for email addresses from your fans and customers. Put a sign-up sheet on your counter or ask for sign-ups on your Facebook page or Twitter. Tell folks you will return the favor with future email offers and discounts for loyal fans. Everyone likes to get offers from brands they trust. Win-win. (Chapter 4 has tips on creating emails.)

No robo-calls. There's nothing like getting a blind, automated phone call from someone trying to sell you something. It is one of the more annoying and intrusive advertising tricks I can think of. You don't want people to think of your brand as annoying. Do you?

Your business is unique and your advertising plan should be too.

You have options. We've covered a lot. Now you have a better idea what's involved with making different kinds of advertising. I'd encourage you to go with whatever works for you. There is no formula. For example, you may want to hire freelance talent to do a magazine ad for you while taking on Google search ads yourself. You may choose to skip radio; that's fine too.

Test and learn. Try staggered launch dates for different kinds of ads—there is no rule that everything must start on the same day. Placing different ads over time is an opportunity to track the start date of each type of ad to actual sales. Once many different ad formats are all running at the same time, it can be a bit more challenging to tell which ads are working the hardest.

 If an ad is not helping to sell products, it might be what's in it. The message may not be as compelling or clear as it could be. Give a different message a try. If it still doesn't work, that type of ad may not work with your customers. What works great for one business may not work for another. That's why there are so many different options. Try something new until you find advertising gold.

When to hire an ad agency.

Most people have no idea that a few million dollars is a tiny budget to make, and then play a commercial on prime-time TV. Big time advertising campaigns are expensive. If you are big time, you should probably hire a creative ad agency. And ask them for an integrated advertising plan to run ad messages in other places besides TV, as well. This is the role of the ad agency: to cover all those bases for you. *Advertising Age* magazine has an online directory link listing top ad agencies you could explore: adage.com/directory.

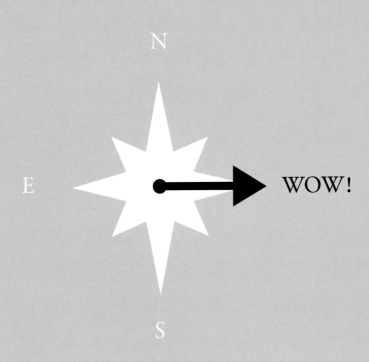

Chapter 6   Find It Here

Whether you're in a small remote town or a big city, you can use these online resources to get the job done. All of the recommendations mentioned throughout this book are listed in this chapter. For the record, I'm not paid by any of these businesses for my endorsements. They do a nice job and are worthy of consideration. Good luck!

Search and buy website addresses aka URLs: Page 5
GoDaddy.com

Find graphics software and typefaces: Page 11
Adobe.com

Hire a logo designer or graphic designer: Page 13
Elance.com

Search for logo trademark conflicts: Page 18
Images.google.com

Trademark or register a logo: Page 19
uspto.gov

Find stock images and graphics: Page 32
iStock.com

Order custom printed business cards and stationery: Page 34
Vistaprint.com
Overnightprints.com

Order fancy letterpress business cards and stationery: Page 34
Eggpress.com

Create and send promotional emails: Page 35
MailChimp.com

Order custom T-shirts, drinkware, mouse pads and more: Page 35
Zazzle.com
Cafepress.com

Create a simple website yourself: Page 37
Weebly.com

Create a YouTube channel: Page 37
YouTube.com/create_channel

Hire a professional web builder and maintenance team: Page 38
Web.com

Learn about website content management options: Page 38
Wordpress.com
Joomla.com

Hire a freelance web designer: Page 39
Elance.com

Create an online store: Page 39
Ebay.com
Etsy.com

Collect online payments via Paypal: Page 39
Paypal.com

Find a Top Digital Agency: Page 39
Topinteractiveagencies.com

Offer customer "check in" apps: Page 41
Foursquare.com
Facebook Places (https://www.facebook.com/about/location)

Join social networks: Page 42-43
Facebook.com
Google.com/+/business

Start micro blogging: Page 43
Twitter.com

Share videos and images: Page 42-43
YouTube.com
Instagram.com
Pinterest.com
Vine-videos.com

Create a blog related to your business: Page 48
Wordpress.com
Blogger.com
Typepad.com
Tumblr.com

Hire a freelance SEO search expert: Page 46
Elance.com

Create Google search ads: Page 46
Google.com/adwords

Share customer reviews online: Page 46
Yelp.com

Hire a freelance creative team to make ads: Page 48
LinkedIn.com

Find passionate new customers in your category: Page 48
Amazon.com/magazines

Find a big time ad agency: Page 51
Adage.com/directory

Share copies of this book with others. Thanks!
DIYBrandDesignBook.com

Your time is limited,
so don't waste it
living someone else's life.
—Steve Jobs

I'll drink to that.
—Gabrielle Weinman

Gabrielle Weinman

Asked to pick between advertising and design majors at Art Center College of Design, Gabrielle picked both — a bit unusual at the time. Little did she know how fortuitous the choice would be. Two weeks after graduation she got her first job at Keith Bright & Associates designing corporate identities for brands in various categories, including cruise lines and overnight shipping. She was even able help save the planet by designing the Heal the Bay logo, which is still in use today.

Gabrielle moved on to become a print designer for Lexus automobiles. After a few short years the Internet was born, and so was her role in founding the digital creative practice at Team One Advertising. Starting from scratch in a totally new discipline, she used both her advertising and design training to create award-winning campaigns lauded with Effies, Clios and One Show Award pencils.

Not able to fit another Lexus sample in her overstuffed portfolio, Gabrielle was lured away by new opportunities, big titles and new brands to work on. Most recently she held the title of EVP, Chief Digital Creative Director at Dailey Advertising. Yet the desire to build a brand of her own based on helping others is what inspires her today.

Made in the USA
Lexington, KY
06 August 2019